JEHOVAH-JIREH
IS HIS NAME

LEONARD W. DeWITT, D.D.

Illustrated by Wendell Dowling

Edited by Grace Pettifor

Copyright 1990
by Bethel Publishing
Elkhart, In 46516
All Rights Reserved
ISBN 0-934998-41-8

Printed in U.S.A.

This book is dedicated to the glory of the Lord who has so faithfully met my needs and to the edification of all who may happen to read it. My prayer is that you, too, will experience God's faithfulness in every area of your life.

TABLE OF CONTENTS

FOREWORD

On the following pages, the reader is given an opportunity to see the marvelous working and moving of God in the life of a man who was sent from God to activate, in a variety of ministries, the plan and will of God. Our interest is drawn from the man behind the pulpit to the man's ministries at home with the family, with major problems and frightening needs. He permits us to observe him walking the paths of men where there are needs — needs for money, for healing, for comfort, and needs for guidance in making major decisions of life-changing importance.

He takes us with him into his closet of prayer where he and God decide the course of action and the method of accomplishment as they deal with issues of major importance.

He shares with us his agony of grief and the divine comfort and provision. Financial needs are met through miraculous provision. Terminal illness is exchanged for vibrant health. And, through it all, God gets the glory.

Yes, on the pages of this book, you will see that JEHOVAH-JIREH is truly "The Lord our Provider."

Leonard DeWitt's life, influence and ministry have truly taught me what it means to be sent from God. Through his ministry God has taught me what it means to truly and consistently walk with God, whatever the cost.

Dr. C. Leslie Miller

INTRODUCTION

Why would anyone write a book entitled <u>JEHO-VAH-JIREH is His Name</u>? This is one of the names of our great God and it means "The Lord our Provider."

At a time when there there is so much gloom and doom, I believe some good news is greatly needed. This small volume is intended to bring encouragement to each one who reads it.

As I have looked back across the years, I have personally experienced intimacy with God. My spirit has been refreshed again and again by God's love, personal concern, response to prayer, specific guidance and generous provision.

I do not view the author as anyone special. The Bible says, "God is no respecter of persons" (Acts 10:34 KJV). He sends rain (blessings) on the just and the unjust. My hope is that <u>JEHOVAH-JIREH is His Name</u> will bring joy to your heart and that you will have the courage to trust him with every area of your life. Our God is an awesome God and He cares about each of us. He knows when a small sparrow falls to the ground. He knows the number of hairs on your head and mine. Our God is not stingy. He is generous and He wants us to trust Him. In Hebrews 11:6 we read, "But without faith it is impossible to please Him, for he who comes to God must believe that He is, and that He is a rewarder of those who diligently seek Him" (NKJV). I pray that each of us will regularly look to our generous God to meet the needs of our lives.

I am grateful to my administrative assistant, Fay De Mars, for her patience in typing and retyping this manuscript. Her insight and response has been most encouraging. Also, I am thankful to the Lord for the friendship, partnership and editorial gifts of Dr. C. Leslie Miller. His counsel and wisdom have been a great source of comfort to me across the years as we have labored together in the Lord's work. His editorial skills have made this volume much more readable and I'm grateful.

Happy reading, dear friends. May each of you find the Lord to be your Provider.

A fellow pilgrim,
Leonard W. DeWitt

ONE
OLD DUKE

"The Lord is my strength and my shield; My heart trusted in Him, and I am helped; Therefore my heart greatly rejoices, And with my song I will praise Him" (Psalm 28:7 NKJV).

What I am about to share is more than a boy's love for an old horse. It is really an account of God's protection.

I grew up on a farm in the province of Alberta in Western Canada. Until I was twelve years old, we used horses to do most of our farm work. "Old Duke" was the name we affectionately tagged to the horse our family used to pull our buggy. Until we bought our first car, an old Model T Ford, the buggy was our primary means of transportation except for winter, when we used an enclosed sleigh.

One summer Sunday, Old Duke was taking my family (except my dad) home from Sunday School and church. We were about one mile out of town when he suddenly stopped. No amount of coaxing by my mother could persuade that horse to take one more step forward. In fact he began to back up and, with unbelievable skill, he maneuvered the buggy and our family off the road and down into the ditch. It's hard to imagine a big rig driver could have done

—W. Dowling

"Old Duke" JEHOVAH-JIREH IS HIS NAME, BY LEONARD DEWITT

any better.

Moments later our attention was drawn to a loud roar and a cloud of dust coming from the direction we had just traveled. Suddenly, two cars racing side by side on that narrow dirt road thundered by. If we had still been on the road, in all likelihood we would have been seriously injured or killed. One of the drivers stopped, came back and checked to see if we were okay. By then Old Duke had skillfully pulled us back up on the road, ready to take us on home.

My mother assured the man we were okay but no thanks to him. He asked our forgiveness and told how he had witnessed our wonder horse deftly removing us from the path of danger. He said, "Someone was surely watching over you."

How did Old Duke know of the danger speeding our way from behind us? How did he know what to do?

Throughout my life I have repeatedly witnessed God as my Protector. The Psalmist says that the Lord is my "hiding place and my shield" (Psalm 119:114 NKJV).

Old Duke will always be a cherished memory. I marvel and rejoice in God's provision of watchful care and protection. The twenty-third Psalm sums it up correctly: "I will fear no evil for Thou art with me" (Psalm 23:4 KJV).

Friend, be of good cheer. Our Heavenly Father is watching over you today.

TWO
YOUR DAD IS DYING

When I was in high school, the Lord was really speaking to me about going into the ministry. I knew he was asking me for a commitment.

One Sunday as we were getting ready for Sunday School and church, my mother informed us that she would be staying home because my father was ill. When we came home, dad was worse. We carried him out and put him in my brother's car. They headed for the hospital.

At the end of that long, tense afternoon, my younger brother and I did the chores and then walked the three miles to town to see what had become of my father and the rest of the family. As we stepped into the hospital corridor, my mother was coming toward us. She broke into tears and said, "Son, your dad had a heart attack. He is in a coma and won't live through the night."

I had been less than an ideal son. My prodigal heart had caused both my parents considerable pain and grief. Now it appeared I would never be able to ask his forgiveness. Even worse, my dad was at death's door and he was not a Christian.

That night the people in the small Missionary Church in our town spent most of the time in the evening service praying for my dad. That same evening, my battle with God's will came to an end and I promised our Lord He could use my life in any way He desired.

Are you ready for this? In the early hours of the next morning, our God sovereignly healed my dad! I will never forget going to his room early that morning and hearing voices. Can you imagine my surprise and joy when I opened the door and saw father sitting up in bed talking to my mother and being examined by the doctor? When the examination was completed, the doctor, who was not a Christian, said, "This is a miracle. I had nothing to do with it. Someone much bigger than me took care of this problem."

No words could describe the joy that came to our family that day. A compassionate Lord healed my father and gained the victory in my life at the same time.

Do you wonder why I love the prayer of Job in chapter 42, verses 1 and 2? He said, "Lord, I know that you can do all things; no plan of yours can be thwarted" (NIV).

Oh, yes, my dad surrendered his life to Christ while I was in college studying for the ministry. Our God reigns and He is able to do immeasurably more than we can ask or think. Dare to be bold in reaching out to Him with each of your concerns. (Romans 8:28-29).

THREE
A HILL OF BEANS

"But you, O Israel, My servant, Jacob, whom I have chosen...You are My servant; I have chosen you and have not rejected you" (Isaiah 41:8-9 NIV).

"The word of the Lord came to me saying, 'Before I formed you in the womb I knew you, before you were born, I set you apart; I appointed you as a prophet to the nations'" (Jeremiah 1:4-5 NIV).

What do you see as a common thread in each of these passages? I see a sovereign God with a plan and purpose for every life.

I was quite young when I sensed the stirring of the Holy Spirit in my heart indicating the Lord had a plan and purpose for my life. The Spirit deeply impressed on my mind that one day I would be a minister of the gospel.

Even though my family lived on a quarter section of good farmland in Western Canada, we never had much of the world's possessions or pleasures. I am sure many other families in our small community had their struggles too. We used to listen with a certain envy when our friends would tell us about vacations they took or gifts they received. There were no vacations or birthday parties when we were growing up. At Christmas we usually received articles of much-needed clothing for which we were grateful but there weren't many toys.

By the time I was seventeen years of age and ready to graduate from high school, I knew that a battle was raging inside over God's call on my life. I loved the Lord but the only ministers I knew didn't seem to have very much and I wanted to do something important and make some big money. I had always enjoyed debating in school and had a strong desire to become a trial lawyer. Thus, in all my planning, I started moving in that direction even though I knew in my heart I was grieving the Lord.

Just weeks before graduating from high school, the manager of the bank in a neighboring town sent word he wanted to see me. I had no idea what he wanted. All I knew was I didn't owe him any money and I was quite sure he wasn't planning to give me any.

I will never forget the day I was ushered into his big, impressive office and invited to be seated in front of his desk. He shared how they had been doing some checking on my academic standing and felt that I could have a terrific future in banking. His proposal was for me to join them upon graduation and they would send me to bankers' college. The bank would pay all the costs. At the end of one year, they would bring me back to the local branch and train me beginning on the bottom rung of the ladder. He assured me that if I worked hard, the day would come when I would have my own branch to manage.

What a dilemma! Here was the opportunity of a lifetime being offered to me on a silver platter. People in banking were usually respected. They had job security and were able to help others. As I was listening to his offer, a little voice was saying to me, "Leonard, this is not My will for you." At the same time, I was planning on pursuing a career in law. Life seemed so complicated at that moment. The manager said, "I want you to take the next two weeks to think it over; then give me your answer."

For the next two weeks I prayed but God had already made it very clear what He wanted me to do with my life, so He didn't seem inclined to give me any further counsel. I actually hoped the Lord would return before I had to go back and give that man my answer. Two weeks later I found myself sitting in the same office in the same chair. Knowing our family, the bank manager knew that he was giving me the opportunity of a lifetime, so he didn't even ask what my decision was. He laid several forms in front of me. Handing me a pen, he said, "Sign each place where it is marked with an X," and he turned to other matters. I sat there with my heart pounding like a sledge hammer. I knew I would be disobeying the Lord if I signed those papers, so I laid the pen down. When the manager looked up and saw I wasn't writing, he wanted to know if there was something wrong with the proposal. I told him everything was fine but that the offer just wasn't for me.

I could tell he was a bit irritated and he posed the

"The Hill of Beans" JEHOVAH-JIREH IS HIS NAME, BY LEONARD DEWITT

very question I was hoping he wouldn't ask, "What are you going to do with your life?"

Very softly I said, "I think some day I'm going to be a minister."

He stood up, very angry, and said, "You young fool! I'm sorry I ever wasted my time on you because you won't amount to a hill of beans. There's the door. Get out."

A strange thing happened as I left that office. I felt really humiliated by all he said and yet, I felt like I had taken a giant step forward. Somehow I knew that, even though I was still struggling with God's will, I had pleased Him with my decision. I discovered through that experience that each time you take a step of obedience you become stronger spiritually and your joy level increases.

I am now completing thirty years of ministry and I can't imagine myself ever doing anything else with my life. What a privilege it has been to serve the Lord and His people and know I am using my life in the exact way He has ordained.

You know, that bank manager was right. I never did become a hill of beans but I thank the Lord for the way He has given me so much peace, purpose and pleasure as I have used my life in the way He directed. There really is joy in serving Jesus.

FOUR
BRAIN DEAD

When God told Abraham and Sarah that they were going to have a son of their very own, they questioned how in their advanced years such a thing could be possible. God's response was in the form of a question, "Is anything too hard for the Lord?" (Genesis 18:14 NIV).

We live in a very self-serving, self-sufficient society. We are used to working things out by ourselves for ourselves. Yet I am convinced that each of us needs to be put in a position where we have positive proof that there isn't anything too hard for the Lord.

Such experiences can come upon us with little or no warning. In May of 1963, Barbara, my first wife, and I celebrated six wonderful years of marriage. We had been blessed with a precious daughter and wonderful son. The Lord honored us as we pastored our first church. After being there three years, I tendered my resignation to go on to seminary. A few weeks later Barbara became ill. At first, the symptoms were like the stomach flu. However, when it continued for a couple of days, our doctor asked us to meet him at the hospital. After some preliminary tests, he decided to keep her there and call in a specialist.

I'll never forget the next day when Dr. G____, the specialist, showed me the X-ray of her cranium and, pointing to a particular spot, said, "I think she has a brain tumor and, if I'm right, it's inoperable because we can't get to it."

The old Gospel song states it so simply, "Where could I go but to the Lord?" Humanly there was no help or hope. During the eight weeks she was hospitalized, she clung to life by a thread. Thousands of people prayed. I wept and cried out to God for her to be spared.

One Sunday morning, just as it was time for the service to begin, the hospital called with the message, "Your wife is dying. Come at once." We lived two blocks away. I ran down the street, into the hospital and up to her room. It was crowded with nurses, doctors and technicians working frantically. I waited in the hall, weeping and praying.

About thirty minutes later the doctor came and said, "She had a massive stroke. Her heart stopped. We finally got it going again. Even if every other problem was worked out, she'd be just a vegetable. Your wife is brain-dead." Personally I think the situation is comparable in challenge to telling Abraham and Sarah in their old age that they were going to have a son. Is anything too hard for the Lord?

For the next week or more she just lay there, her heart beating but no response of any kind to their periodic tests.

On a rotating basis several friends joined me in sitting at her bedside reading passages of Scripture out loud and praying. I was there the afternoon her doctor came by and ran a pointed instrument up the soles of her feet. We both saw her toes move. He said, "I don't believe it!" He repeated the test several times with her feet and hands with the same results. Each day her reflexes were sharper. About a week after the first response she opened her eyes and there was recognition.

Barbara made great strides in the following days. They had her sitting on the edge of her bed, then in a chair, and finally up walking and pushing her wheelchair around. There was no damage of any kind. Her doctor, a brilliant neuro-surgeon, told me, "You folks have a power I don't know anything about."

She had three terrific weeks and the doctor was getting ready to send her home when there were small signs of regression. Almost a week later she went back into a coma. A week after that, our Lord called her home.

My heart cry to God was, "Why? Why did you bring her all the way back from brain-dead and then turn around and take her?"

The message He impressed on my heart and mind was, "So that you would never question what I can do. I wanted you to see for yourself that there isn't anything too hard for Me."

I don't pretend to understand all of God's ways. It was tough losing my friend, lover and companion of six years. However, there is one thing I know

24

for sure, my friend: there is nothing too hard for our Lord. He is able to do "exceedingly abundantly above all that we ask or think" (Ephesians 3:20 KJV).

I hope you will discover this for yourself.

FIVE
SENSE OUT OF SORROW

A favorite passage of Scripture to me is 2 Corinthians 1:3-4 where we read, "Praise be to the God and Father of our Lord Jesus Christ, the Father of compassion and the God of all comfort, who comforts us in all of our troubles, so that we can comfort those in any trouble with the comfort we ourselves have received from God" (NIV).

Have you ever considered some of the things that happened to you and wondered, "What good could possibly come out of this?" That's how I felt that hot, July afternoon, standing in the corridor of St. Joseph's Hospital in Yakima, Washington. Dr. Gottlieb said, "Your wife just died."

It was hard to believe this was happening to me. After all, I was a clergyman. I was serving the Lord. What about our two very young children? What about their need for a mother? A million questions pierced my grief as I stood there hearing his words but not comprehending all it would mean.

In addition to the loss of my loved one, I received a letter from the hospital insurance company. They maintained that my wife's condition was pre-existent at the time I took out the policy. Suddenly

I was faced with all the medical costs with no money in the bank. At that point, I began to feel a bit like Job and wondered where the next bad news would come from.

I had no choice but to throw myself totally upon the Lord. Psalm 34:4 pictures the Psalmist saying, "I sought the Lord, and He answered me; He delivered me from all my fears" (NIV). As I cried out to the Lord, He reached out to me.

A man came to me just hours after my wife died and gave me a cemetery plot in the most beautiful memorial gardens in the area.

My sister contacted me and stated, "I want to come and help you and the children for at least a year."

About two years later, I was pastoring in another city. A funeral director said, "Pastor, I know you have personally experienced a great loss. Yet you seem to have come through victoriously. Many of the people we serve have no pastor, no church and no hope. I was wondering if, out of your own experience, you would be willing to help them?"

Suddenly a light went on! I could see my situation as a bridge I could walk across into other peoples' lives.

In the years that followed, the church I was pastoring was largely built on a ministry to bereaved, hurting families.

Dear friends, "God understands your heartache, He sees each falling tear and whispers 'I am with you, then falter not nor fear.'"

Our God can make sense out of your situation and give you a ministry to others you never dreamed possible.

SIX
A GOOD IDEA, HUH, DADDY

How do you feel when a close friend or member of your family dies? I am sure that our acceptance of it is determined to some degree by our own faith and hope in the hereafter. We also are comforted if the loved one was a believer. To have a loved one die who was not a Christian can be very tough because we know that where a person will spend eternity is determined by that person's relationship with the Son of God.

In John 5:24 our Lord said, "Most assuredly, I say to you, he who hears My word and believes in Him who sent Me has everlasting life, and shall not come into judgment, but has passed from death into life" (NKJV).

We read further in 1 John 5:11-13, "And this is the testimony: that God has given us eternal life, and this life is in His Son. He who has the Son has life; he who does not have the Son of God does not have life. These things I have written to you who believe in the name of the Son of God, that you may know that you have eternal life" (NKJV).

In 1963, when my first wife was in the hospital and her condition was critical, I was praying and asking our Lord to show me what He wanted. One day as I was reading my Bible, my eyes rested on Psalm 116:15, "Precious in the sight of the Lord is the death of His saints" (KJV). At that moment I knew that God intended to call her home to heaven. I wept over the prospect of being alone without her love. A few days later she was ushered into the presence of the Lord she loved.

When I came home from the hospital I wondered how I would ever be able to help our three-year-old daughter and ten-month-old son understand what had just happened. I took our daughter out in the front yard and sat on an old stump, holding her on my lap. We talked about how sick her mother had been. She had seen the bandages and had witnessed that her mother was not her usual vibrant self. I assured her that Jesus loves each of us and that he wasn't satisfied to just leave her mother in the hospital to suffer. Then I told her how, just a few minutes earlier, our Lord had called Barbara home to be with Him. Finally, I assured her that He was getting things ready for us too and that, at just the right time, He would send for us also.

As I looked into Pam's young face to see if she comprehended what I had told her, I saw a tear form in the corner of each eye and then, suddenly, a smile spread all across her face and she said, "That's a good idea, huh, daddy!" How good of our Lord to flood her young heart with such understanding.

All I could do for Sheldon was hold him close, tell him how much we all loved him and assure him that one day he would understand how special it is to have a loved one, even your mother, safely home in heaven. The Apostle Paul said, "For I am hard pressed between the two, having a desire to depart and be with Christ, which is far better" (Philippians 1:23 NKJV).

These many years later with both of our children grown, knowing and loving the Lord, they have a shared conviction: "That's a good idea, huh, daddy!"

Dear friend, are you personally facing death? Do you have a loved one who is critically ill? Perhaps you have a mate or a child who is already with the Lord. Do you understand, as a Christian, that most of our grief is for ourselves? What could be better than absent from the body and present with the Lord?

My precious reader, God's ways may twist and turn but one thing is certain...He makes no mistakes. He wants us home with Him. That's a great idea!

SEVEN
A NEW BEGINNING

From the time I married in 1957 and moved from
Western Canada to Washington State, I thrived on
the friendship and companionship we shared. We
were friends as well as lovers and it was
wonderful. I was counting on our celebrating at
least a golden anniversary and maybe much more.
Then suddenly, a few weeks after our sixth
anniversary, death invaded our world and I was
alone and lonely.

Perhaps some people enjoy being alone but I am
not one of them. To this day my heart aches for
those who are alone. The worst loneliness of all is
that which is caused by divorce. When separation is
caused by death, it's final. However, when
separation is caused by divorce, it is never over.

It seems that there are stages in life and the
Christian has a great advantage over the non-
Christian. In Christ we have a Friend who sticks
closer to us than a brother. I marvel over the way
He is all-knowing and wise. He anticipates our
every need and is prepared to meet it.

When Barbara died in 1963, I was suddenly left
alone with two very young children, thousands of
dollars of doctors' bills and a lot of questions.

"A New Beginning" JEHOVAH-JIREH IS HIS NAME, BY LEONARD DEWITT

There was no way I could hire a housekeeper. If she was too young, people would talk and if she was too old, she wouldn't have the stamina to keep up.

About two weeks had passed and I was pondering my options when my only sister called. She said, "I have just graduated from college and have been on my job for a few weeks. As I have been praying for you and the children, the Lord has impressed on me that I should offer to come and help you. So, Leonard, if you need me I will be happy to come and be with you for a year."

Can you imagine the joy that filled my heart? Suddenly I realized what Job meant when he said, "The Lord gave, and the Lord has taken away; Blessed be the name of the Lord" (Job 1:21 NKJV).

A new excitement filled my heart because I knew God had not abandoned me. His words in the prophecy of Isaiah meant so much to me: "I will go before you and make the crooked places straight" (Isaiah 45:2 NKJV). Even though His ways were higher and different than mine, I knew I could trust Him with every situation and decision. "For My thoughts are not your thoughts, nor are your ways My ways, says the Lord. For as the Heavens are higher than the earth, so are My ways higher than your ways, and My thoughts than your thoughts" (Isaiah 55:8-9 NKJV).

He showed me that the best thing I could do was fix my eyes on Him and He would fill my heart with His peace. "You will keep in perfect peace him whose mind is steadfast, because he trusts in You" (Isaiah 26:3 NIV). As I waited on Him my strength was renewed and my spirit revived. "Those who hope in the Lord will renew their strength. They will soar on wings like eagles; they will run and not grow weary, they will walk and not be faint" (Isaiah 40:31 NIV).

My sister, Opal, is truly a gem. She is precious in God's sight and mine. Can you see how completely in control God really was? What if she had been married and had her own family to care for? It would have been impossible for her to help. She stayed with us more than a year. What a blessing she was in our lives and also to the people I was pastoring.

Friend, you may be at a crossroad in your life. It all looks so helpless and hopeless. Remember, Christ is our Shepherd and He knows which way to take. His invitation to you is, "Come to Me all you who labor and are heavy laden, and I will give you rest" (Matthew 11:28 NKJV). He never fails to give it.

This can be the first day of your new beginning. Don't look for a way out of your situation. Look to Jesus. Listen for Him to speak. Be quick to do what He asks and enjoy a brand new chapter in your life.

EIGHT
MISSING: ONE INSURANCE POLICY

Have you ever lost or misplaced something that you desperately needed? Do you recall the urgency that spurred you on in your search? Hopefully, you found the item in question. What were your emotions when you located the lost item?

In Luke 15, the Savior shares three parables with the people. They focus on the lost sheep, the lost silver and the lost son. Each parable reveals the concern of the parent and owners and the celebration that took place when the lost was found. We see in these accounts a beautiful picture of the stubborn love that our Heavenly Father has for each of us.

In 1958, my wife and I were in Bible College and we were running low on funds. Somehow I had to reduce our expenses. We decided to cancel my wife's life insurance policy and notified the company accordingly. At the end of each college year, we went back to Yakima, Washington, for the summer months to try and earn enough to get us through the next period of preparation. By the time we graduated in 1960 and returned to Washington State to pastor our first church, we had moved several times. Each time I threw away things we no longer needed.

Between 1958 and 1963 we never had any communication with the insurance company that had carried Barbara's policy. By the same token, I didn't expect any for I had cancelled the coverage. Early in 1963 I received a letter from them which didn't make much sense. Since I didn't have any more money than when I was in college, I dropped it in the trash.

Several months later, Barbara became ill without any warning. She was hospitalized and many tests led the doctors to the conclusion that she had an inoperable brain tumor.

I lived a lifetime in the next two months. She had several operations and was faced with many complications. Most of the eight weeks Barbara was in the hospital, her condition was critical. Her health deteriorated as the medical costs sky-rocketed. Then the Lord called her home. At the end, they learned that the real culprit was a very rare type of meningitis.

There is a real empathy in my heart for Job. How quickly he was stripped of everything. That's how I felt. I faced thousands of dollars in doctor and hospital costs. My wife, whom I dearly loved, was taken from me. The company that carried our hospitalization told me my wife's condition was pre-existent to when the coverage went into effect. They never paid one cent. Two very small children missed their mother terribly. One of my main concerns was, "How am I going to pay these bills?"

As I was praying about this one day, I felt strongly impressed by the Holy Spirit to write to the company that had carried Barbara's life insurance. I couldn't believe how strongly I felt led to contact them. At the same time, I was embarrassed. "What kind of nut will they think I am?" I wondered. I hadn't paid a premium in over five years and now I'm wondering what is the status of the policy. Each time I prayed for wisdom, the answer was the same, "Write to the insurance company!"

Finally it came down to a matter of obedience and I wrote the letter. Several weeks later the reply nearly knocked me off my chair. "Because of the automatic premium-paying clause in the policy, the coverage has been maintained. This will remain in force for several more months. By then we feel you will be in a position to care for the premiums personally. At present, the policy is worth $2390.00." Can you believe that! I had never heard of such a thing. It was a long way from covering all the costs but it would surely help.

I turned the letter over to my attorney and he contacted them about payment. They said they would be happy to pay but I had to surrender the policy. My heart sank. I was frustrated because I was sure that I had thrown the policy away several months after we cancelled the coverage. Here I stood a chance of receiving funds and yet they seemed a million miles away, all because of a missing policy.

A few days later I got up early one morning and went to my office for prayer. As I stood in front of the old bookcase with the glass doors and drawers at the bottom, my mind was flooded with, "Lord, what are you doing to me? I overcame my pride and wrote the insurance company. Much to my surprise there was money available. Now I can't get it because I threw away the stupid policy. God, why?"

Without even thinking about what I was doing, I bent over and opened one of the drawers. There right on top was the missing insurance policy! I don't think Moses at the Red Sea could have experienced any more joy or excitement as the waters parted. I could see my sea of despair beginning to part and I knew Jehovah-Jireh was providing for a badly hurting family.

Friend, God is no respecter of persons. He doesn't love me more than He loves you. He may ask you to do some things that seem very strange but your obedience can help you experience the mighty hand of God meeting your need. What adventure lies ahead to all who trust Him!

NINE
FORTUNE COOKIES

I first met Joyce in 1960 when my wife and I moved to Yakima, Washington, to begin our pastoral ministry. The church had gone through a split and had actually been closed for a period of time. Then a retired minister opened it again. In time his health began to fail, so the small congregation contacted me and wanted to know if I would come and be their pastor when I graduated from Bible College. My beginning salary was fifty dollars a month. This meant that I would have to seek other employment.

Someone told me the Salvation Army was looking for a truck driver and all-purpose worker. While I was quite sure the income there would not be large, I felt they would understand if I needed time off for a conference, funeral, etc. They hired me and I worked for them for eight months. Joyce, a bookkeeper by profession, was hired by them to care for all their records.

As I got to know her, I was deeply impressed with her love for the Lord. She had a beautiful shyness about her and would even laugh at my jokes. I could hardly believe that some sharp, godly young man had not won her heart and hand

for life. At times I would even encourage single
men I knew to stop by and meet her. My intention
was for them to ask her out. It didn't take long for
her to realize what was going on. In her own way
she let me know what she thought of "my help."

Sometime after my wife died, a mutual friend of
Joyce and myself thought we should at least date
and see if we might have a future together. In my
heart I was still very much married. The thought
of trying to start over was so scary. I couldn't
imagine any woman who would be willing to
become a wife, mother and pastor's wife all in one
leap.

Our mutual friend continued to try and play cupid
month after month but I resisted. I knew that if I
asked Joyce out and she refused, then I would be too
embarrassed to continue stopping by the office to
visit. One day, however, our friend called me a
coward and that was the last straw. Under a lot of
stress, I stopped by to see Joyce and finally got my
invitation out. Much to my surprise, she said,
"Yes." Later, I learned that she thought a group
was going and our being together would not be too
noticeable. When she found that was not the case,
she was scared but followed through on her
promise.

Somehow we both survived that first date. She
even consented to go out with me again. On our
third date we went for Chinese food. When they
brought our fortune cookies at the end of the meal,
something happened that we have been laughing
about ever since.

Her little slip of paper had one word on it: "Triplets." She was being forewarned that if she pursued this friendship she might wind up with a threesome to care for. My slip of paper said: "Cottage and Carriage." The first parsonage we would live in was a cottage and my son was still young enough that he was in a carriage.

Let me hasten to say that neither one of us depends on fortune cookies for divine guidance. However, through the years we have had fun watching the expressions on people's faces when we say, "Let us tell you how God used fortune cookies to reveal His will to us."

I never cease to be amazed at the way our Heavenly Father directs our lives. The Bible says that "The steps of a good man (woman) are ordered by the Lord" (Psalm 37:23 KJV).

A year after we were married Joyce became very ill and would have died if they had not conducted exploratory surgery. They found many things wrong inside. There was no choice but to do a complete hysterectomy. What a blow that was because both of us wanted to have children. However, the Lord made the two little ones I brought into the relationship even more special to her and they love her dearly. If she had married a man without children, it is highly questionable if they could ever have adopted children because her health problems are still lingering after twenty-five years.

We have found His ways to be accompanied by His grace and it gets better and better each year.

As the Psalmist said in 16:5-6, we have found it true in our lives: "O Lord, You are the portion of my inheritance and my cup; You maintain my lot. The lines have fallen to me in pleasant places; yes, I have a good inheritance" (NKJV).

We are not trusting Chinese fortune cookies for God's goodness. Rather, we are rejoicing in His good favor every step of the way. As the songwriter said, we concur: "I'd rather have Jesus than anything this world affords."

TEN
LICENSE PLATES

I believe God is interested in every area of our lives. In 1 Peter 5:7, the Apostle Peter wrote, "Cast all your anxiety on Him because He cares for you" (NIV).

Many times our mindset is, "I don't want to trouble the Lord with such a small matter. He has better things to do. I will handle this myself and just come to Him with the crisis matters." Such an approach to life may seem noble but it denies God access into all areas of our lives and displays a certain arrogance as well.

Since our Lord knows how many hairs are on our heads or when a sparrow falls to the ground, why wouldn't He be interested in even the small concerns we have?

When my wife and I were married, we each had a vehicle with many miles registered and we were spending more and more on repairs. As we prayed for wisdom, it seemed to us we would be better off to dispose of both vehicles and get reliable transportation within our means. In time we purchased a lovely Buick Skylark. We enjoyed that car very much.

Then January came and it was time to get our new

license tabs. That year they would cost us fifty-three dollars. When you don't have it, even a small amount makes a lasting impression on your memory. My strategy was to put aside twenty-five percent of the amount each week so that by the last day of the month I would have the funds in hand. Wouldn't you know that in January we were faced with one expense after another? When we came to the end of the month, we had three dollars in the bank. Talk about pressure. The next day I couldn't drive our car for fear of being arrested.

On that last day, I was on my knees in my office early in the morning asking God for help. Suddenly my mind was filled with, "It will be in the mail." My heart was flooded with peace. I could hardly wait for the mail that morning and when it came, there wasn't one cent. Yet my confidence was steadfast. About 2:30 p.m. the doorbell rang and there stood the mailman with a small package.

When I looked at the name of the sender, it was unfamiliar. Upon opening the package I found a leather-bound packet of postcards. Each one had a stamp on it, ready for use. My first thought was, "Lord, I don't have time to write for help!"

Just then a piece of paper fell out. It was a note from a lady I had met about six months earlier at her mother's funeral in another city. She said she had intended to write every week since I conducted her mother's funeral but in recent weeks she felt a real urgency to do so. The note concluded with, " Please use the attached check for any personal need you may have." It was in the amount of fifty dollars.

Thus, three dollars in the bank plus the check made it possible to get my license.

Friend, God understands your heartache and He cares.

"Roasts"

JEHOVAH-JIREH IS HIS NAME   BY LEONARD DEWITT

ELEVEN
ROASTS

Does God take a personal interest in the food on our tables? It would appear from what the Apostle Paul says that God is open to responding to any legitimate request made by His children.

Years ago my wife and I attended a Pastors' and Wives' Conference. I learned that to attend such opportunities can be very costly. When I asked my wife what her speaker shared, I discovered that she had gleaned some very practical ideas.

One of the ideas the speaker shared was a way Sunday could be less hectic for the first lady of the parsonage. Frequently, by the time we got home from church and my wife fixed dinner and then we cleaned up, it was mid-afternoon.

The creative idea was to put a roast in the oven every Sunday before going to church. We could also cook the vegetables with the roast. By the time we got home from church, dinner would be ready and we would have saved at least an hour.

Now, doesn't that sound like a great idea? The problem we faced was how to put a roast in the oven each Sunday when our hamburger budget was already over-taxed. I could picture how much easier this would be for my very busy wife so we talked it over as a family and decided to ask God for roasts. Several weeks later the phone rang one evening and it was one of the men from our church asking if I liked beef liver. They had just butchered and he invited me to come out early the next morning to pick up the liver. When I arrived at their farm, I was stunned when the man informed me that he was not only giving me the liver but also a front quarter of that beef!

When I got back to town and went to my friend, the butcher, to see what he could do with a front quarter, he said, "Pastor, that is great for roasts and hamburger." Can you imagine that! Well, why wouldn't the God who gave His people water, manna and meat in the wilderness be interested in giving our family roasts to be enjoyed in Washington State?

Friend, Peter has some great counsel for all of us: "Casting all your care upon Him; for He careth for you" (1 Peter 5:7 KJV).

He loves you. Look to Him for your "roasts."

TWELVE
WHERE IS THE LAMB?

In Genesis 22 we read of God asking Abraham to take His son, Isaac, to Mount Moriah and there offer him as a sacrifice to God. This was really a test of Abraham's love for God as compared to his love for his son.

We read in verse three, "So Abraham rose early in the morning...and went to the place of which God had told him" (NKJV).

When they arrived and all was in readiness, Isaac said to his father, "My father!...Look, the fire and the wood, but where is the lamb for a burnt offering?" (v.7 NKJV).

His father replied, "My son, God will provide for Himself the lamb for a burnt offering" (v.8 NKJV).

Of course, if you are familiar with the account, at the last possible moment God told Abraham to release his son and there was a ram caught by his horns in the brush nearby. He was offered in place of Isaac.

In the late 1960's, there was a hepatitis epidemic in the community where I was pastoring. Even though I exercised caution in my contact with our people, somehow I managed to pick up whatever was causing the sickness and I, too, was ill with hepatitis.

Because I did not jaundice, my doctor was not suspicious of my having that illness. Almost two weeks went by and I was getting worse by the hour. In desperation, I went back to the doctor and he determined that I had hepatitis and he sent me directly to the hospital. Later, he told me that my infectious count was so high that there had been no chance of my surviving. He had sent me to the hospital to die.

People prayed and God answered by sparing my life. Weeks later when the doctor was ready to release me, he told my wife that all they could do was recommend rest and diet. Concerning the latter, he said that lamb would be very good for me. When was the last time you priced lamb in the meat market?

We were a family of four and I was receiving fifty dollars per week. There was no slack in our budget for lamb. A few days before I was released, my wife came to visit me all excited. No one knew a word about the doctor's recommended diet. One of the men in our church had a flock of about thirty sheep. His wife called to say they had just taken one of their young ones to the butcher and it would be cut and wrapped and ready for us in just a few days! No wonder the songwriter was inspired to write, "My Jesus knows just what I need."

In Genesis 22:14 we read, "And Abraham called the name of the place 'The-Lord-Will-Provide' as it is said to this day, In the mount of the Lord it shall be provided" (NKJV).

Friend, God knows what you need. Look to Him with confidence. Trust Him to provide for you and yours.

THIRTEEN
BE ANNOINTED

Just as a loving parent provides the things that are really needed for his or her children, our Heavenly Father does the same for us.

In Psalm 103 we read, "Bless the Lord, O my soul, and forget not all His benefits: Who *forgives* all your iniquities, Who *heals* all your diseases, Who *redeems* your life from destruction, Who *crowns* you with loving kindness and tender mercies, Who *satisfies* your mouth with good things, so that your youth is renewed like the eagle's" (Verses 2-5 NKJV).

You will notice that one of the benefits our Lord makes available to us is that of healing. In an earlier chapter, I mentioned that years ago I became very ill with hepatitis. When the doctor released me from the hospital he said, "Leonard, you are a workaholic. It is important for you to face the fact that you will never be able to keep the pace you have been used to. The infectious count was so high that some of the organs of your body have been permanently damaged. You will need to learn to live at a much slower pace."

Even though I heard what he was saying, it didn't really register. That did not sink in until several weeks later when he told me I could resume my ministry. I discovered I had almost no stamina. Just to walk across a room left me exhausted and wet with perspiration. Daily I battled depression. After a few months, I was no stronger. I began to fear I would be in this condition the rest of my life.

I grew up with a strong sense of pride and never wanted to be one of those preachers who seemed to work only one day a week. In panic I began to cry out to God not to leave me in my present condition. Each time I prayed about it, there was a persistent inner voice, "Leonard, I want you to obey My word and be anointed with oil according to James 5:13-15. Trust Me to meet your need."

Through the years I had ministered to the sick in this way with some wonderful results. This time, however, it was me. I was afraid that if God didn't come through, it might hurt my people's faith.

The weeks slipped by and I felt no better. In fact, at times I felt worse. One Saturday morning I told the Lord I would obey Him no matter what was the outcome. The very next day, Sunday, I shared with my people how God had been dealing with me. I asked them to pray for me even as our elders came and anointed me.

As you know, throughout the Scriptures, oil symbolizes the Person and ministry of the Holy Spirit. That morning as I was anointed with oil in the name of our Lord my heart was filled with peace and joy. Within six weeks my health and strength were restored and I have been going strong ever since!

With the Psalmist I shout, "Bless the Lord, O my soul, and forget not all His benefits!" (Psalm 103:2 NKJV).

What a great God we have. He cares about you.

FOURTEEN
CALIFORNIA BOUND

Throughout the Bible we see God giving direction to His people. He is a God of purpose and order. I find it personally exciting to be led by the Lord. That is the only reason I am in the ministry today. In unmistakable ways the Lord made very clear to me what He had in mind for my life. "You did not choose Me, but I chose you and appointed you that you should go and bear fruit, and that your fruit should remain, that whatever you ask the Father in My name He may give you" (John 15:16 NKJV).

The second church I pastored was in Wapato, Washington. Located on the Yakima Indian Reservation, it is often referred to as the fruit-bowl of the nation because of all the fruit raised there. Wapato is also called the "Little United Nations" because of the plurality of nationalities. We loved the area and I would have been content to stay there the rest of my life.

During my sixth year, I began to sense that the Lord was going to move us — but where? Several times in the months that followed, other churches contacted us to see if I would come and be their pastor. Each time it was with a sense of relief that

I determined God was not ready to transplant our family. We loved being right where we were.

One day a District Superintendent from another area called to inform me that one of his churches wanted me to come and be their pastor. I was overwhelmed because it was a church I had dreamed of being a part of someday. Now it appeared that day had arrived. When I shared this news with Joyce, she didn't display the excitement I felt. As I pressed her for a response, she said, "Leonard, I will go anywhere with you. Just be sure you aren't putting your personal desires ahead of God's will." Ouch! That really hurt. However, I quickly responded with, "But God knows I have dreamed of pastoring that church and His word says 'He will give us the desires of our hearts.'" She gave me one of those knowing looks. I knew that she was really counting on me to get alone with the Lord and pray this through.

During that week as I searched the Scriptures and prayed for direction, a strange thing happened. The desire to pastor that church began to fade. I did everything I could to revive my dream but I knew I was not to go. Writing those people whom I loved and telling them I couldn't come was one of the hardest things I have ever done. When I released that letter and let it slide through the slot in the post office, my heart was flooded with pure joy. I knew I had pleased the Lord.

But if not there, where? A month later, on a Saturday evening, the telephone rang and a man from a church in Ventura, California, was calling to see if we were open to coming there to pastor. He told me about all the hurt and discouragement the congregation had gone through. As I listened to the bleak picture he painted, a still small voice was saying, "This time you won't be saying no." In many ways over the next couple of weeks, God confirmed to our hearts that He did indeed want us to move to California. It would have been so easy to have insisted on my dream of the other church and missed out on one of the greatest adventures in faith in a lifetime. Thank God for a Scandinavian wife who dared say, "Be careful you don't put your dreams ahead of God's will."

We had the joy of pastoring the Ventura Missionary Church for ten years and saw it grow from one hundred people to over seventeen hundred. To God be the glory! I could never begin to adequately praise the Lord for the privilege of serving Him with such a terrific church family.

He is truly the God who does "exceedingly abundantly above all that we ask or think, according to the power that worketh in us" (Ephesians 3:20 KJV).

FIFTEEN
HOUSE ON VARSITY STREET

I am always amazed at the way God chooses to provide for us. When we moved to Ventura, California in 1971, the church owned a very comfortable parsonage. A big part of our ministry has always been having people in our home. The parsonage was not large so we began to consider buying a house of our own that would have a large living room or family room.

Periodically we would get together with a real estate agent and go looking. I was always relieved when we didn't find what we were looking for. That may sound strange but we did not have any money saved and I could not see how we could ever buy our own home.

This routine continued for the better part of a year. Then one day, on our way back to the agent's office, he asked if we minded stopping so he could see a house that had just come on the market. It was way beyond our price range so he wasn't thinking of us. He wanted to familiarize himself with the house for other clients.

As we walked through it, we realized the house had every feature we were looking for, plus some extras. I was almost afraid to breathe for fear my wife would say, "We'll take it." Please keep in mind that we had been praying for a considerable period of time that the Lord would lead us to the house of His choosing.

When we got home I said to my wife, "That's the house, isn't it?"

She said, "It has everything we want but we can't afford it."

My response was, "You're absolutely right, but if God wants us to have it, He'll work out a way." We agreed as a family to pray daily for two weeks. In my mind I was thinking someone would come along and buy it and that would solve my dilemma.

At the end of two weeks I had no sense of direction so we prayed another two weeks. I never went near the place to see if the *For Sale* sign was still there. Later I learned that my wife went by regularly. I believe she claimed that place. Houses were selling as quickly as they appeared on the market.

When four weeks had passed I woke on a Monday morning, my day off, and I knew the Lord wanted me to make an offer on that house. All my fears were gone. There was just a wonderful sense of peace and adventure. I called our Christian real estate agent and said I was interested in making an offer on the house on Varsity Street.

His response was, "That's very interesting. It's the best house on the market and there has not been one offer on it!" Now I was really excited.

The house had been appraised so the asking price

was the actual value. Having never purchased a house, I felt led to offer eight thousand less than they were asking. The agent nearly had a heart attack and assured me I would never get it for that price. I told him I was willing to come up two thousand dollars but could not go any higher. He called me that evening to say the people were very disappointed in the offer but would think about it overnight. The next day at 5:00 p.m. he came to my office to inform me that my offer was too low and they could not accept it. I was both disappointed and relieved. Then he continued, "They did say, Leonard, that if you would come up one thousand dollars, you could have it. The house is yours!"

Can you imagine the celebrating our family did that night as we worshipped and praised God for our new home? We call it our miracle house. Over the years, many people have entered its doors and we have been blessed by their fellowship.

God's word assures us that our Heavenly Father cares about the birds and flowers and that we are much more important than these. His invitation to us is, "Call unto Me, and I will answer thee, and show thee great and mighty things, which thou knowest not" (Jeremiah 33:3 KJV).

Come visit us at our miracle house on Varsity Street.

SIXTEEN
HONEY, THE REFRIGERATOR...

In the gospel according to John, our Lord said, "And whatever ye shall ask in My name, that will I do, that the Father may be glorified in the Son" (John 14:13 KJV).

When my wife and I were married, I had an old refrigerator that I think Noah used on the ark. Well, that might be a slight exaggeration, but it was old and just limped along. The problem was there was no money for a new one. We prayed that the Lord wouldn't let that refrigerator give out and, for the seven years we pastored in Wapato, Washington, it continued to function.

In 1971, we had moved to California and took 'old faithful' with us. There still was no money to replace it but we knew that the time was coming when we would have no choice. My esteem was taking a beating because I wanted to provide adequately for my family and I could see no way humanly possible to get a new refrigerator. Also, the tires on our car were almost worn out. They were so thin you could nearly see the air. Please note I said 'nearly.' The point is, it wasn't safe to be driving with tires in that condition.

God certainly knew my heart and that I wanted

to be a good provider. Furthermore, I believed that God — Who takes a personal interest in sparrows, flowers and grass — might just care about a refrigerator and tires.

I began to pray and ask the Lord to show me how I might see these needs met. One day my wife said, "Honey, the refrigerator is just barely keeping things cool. It won't keep them cold." I assured her that the Lord was going to help us get a new refrigerator but, inwardly, I wasn't sure how.

For the next few days I continued to present our needs to the Lord. One evening at church, a precious man came up to me and said, "Pastor, how are you doing?" I told him that things were just fine. He said to me, "Are you sure? God has put you on my heart and I felt like maybe I was supposed to help you." At that point my pride stood up and flexed. I had already told Carl that things were just great and my pride wouldn't permit me to tell him otherwise. He walked away shaking his head with a puzzled look on his face.

At that point the Lord began to chide me. "Leonard, you dummy! You have been crying the blues about your refrigerator and tires. I have sent My servant to help you and you send him away. What's the matter with you?"

I realized that I had really blown it and told the Lord I was sorry. Then I said, "Lord, if you intended for Carl to be the answer to my prayers, please send him back."

A few days later Carl met me in the corridor at the church and said, "Pastor, I'm only going to ask you this one time. Do you have any special needs? "

I said, "Carl, I'm sorry for putting you through this. By the time I realized what you were asking me the other evening, I had already told you that things were fine and my pride wouldn't let me tell you otherwise. The truth is, our refrigerator is ready to die and the tires on my car are really worn out."

This dear man's reaction was terrific. He said, "I knew it! I knew it! God told me I was to help you and when you told me things were fine, I could hardly believe it. Pastor, I'll have a check for you tomorrow."

Sure enough, the next day he brought me a check for one thousand dollars! We took out our tithe and gave that to the church. Then, with a great sense of joy, we went shopping. How good the Lord is! He knew before I ever prayed that we had those needs. His word says, "Before they call, I will answer" (Isaiah 65:24 KJV).

We no longer have the car that I put those tires on. However, we do have the refrigerator-freezer. Every time we look at it we see Jehovah-Jireh, The-Lord-Our-Provider. He cares about you and your needs. Don't hesitate to share your concerns with Him. Oh, yes, be sure to praise Him when He answers.

SEVENTEEN
STEVE McQUEEN

"Therefore, if anyone is in Christ, he is a new creation; the old has gone, the new has come!" (2 Corinthians 5:17 NIV).

Across the years, the Lord has put many wonderful people in my life. Frequently I have reflected on how the Devil used to taunt me when I was in high school and struggling with God's call on my life. I had known for several years that the Lord was calling me to follow Him into the ministry. However, Satan would counter with, "If you surrender your life to Him, you'll never go anywhere, see anything, know anyone or have anything." For a young man coming from a very poor background, the enemy's suggestions were hard to ignore. Now, many years later, I can see that saying yes to the call of Christ was the smartest thing I ever did. I feel as if our Lord has been using my life to show the Devil for the liar that he really is.

One Sunday in 1979, we were at home in the afternoon and our children said to me, "Daddy, did you know that Steve McQueen was in church this morning?" Of course I didn't and I began to wonder how he happened to come and worship with us.

Sometime the following week I learned that he had purchased a couple of airplanes and one of our men, Sammy Mason, was giving him flying lessons.

Steve had always been one of my favorite actors. I didn't know much about him personally but I liked the way he portrayed a part in his films. When I heard that he was taking flying lessons from Sammy, I chuckled because I knew that he had met his match. Mr. Mason is not one to ram his religion down your throat. Rather, his faith in Jesus Christ is so much a part of his life that, if you are around him for any length of time, it is going to rub off on you.

It did not take Steve long to realize that Sammy was different from any man he had ever met before. When he was invited to worship with this family some Sunday, it was easy for him to accept. He respected them and felt safe in their company.

This rugged actor liked the church. He asked to be treated like the rest of the congregation. People respected that and did not ask him for autographs. Steve was coming to the house of God to seek the Lord and worship and everyone wanted him to have the privacy he needed.

After he had been attending for several months, he asked if the two of us could have some time together. A few days later we met at the Santa Paula Airport. For two solid hours he fired one question after another about Jesus Christ and the Christian life. Finally, he sat back, smiled and said, "Well, that about covers it for me."

At that point I said, "Steve, I have only one

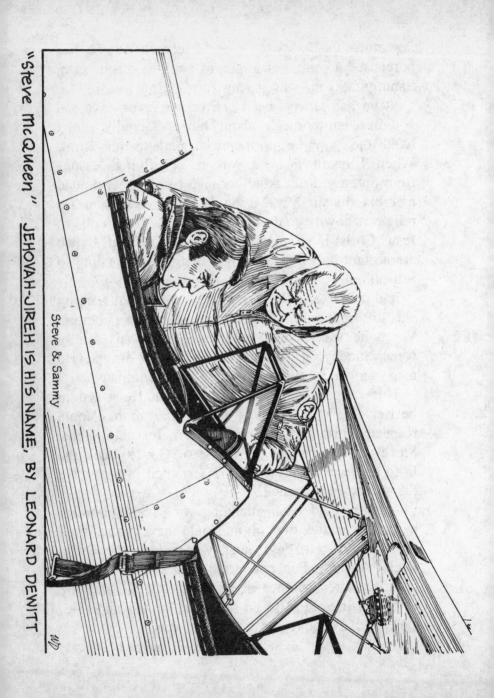

"Steve McQueen" JEHOVAH-JIREH IS HIS NAME, BY LEONARD DEWITT

Steve & Sammy

question to ask you."

He obviously was anticipating this and said, "You want to know if I am a born-again Christian." I assured him that this was my primary interest in him. Then he took me back to a particular Sunday morning when the Holy Spirit had really touched hearts through the message. He said, "When you invited people to pray with you to receive Christ, I prayed and, yes, I'm a born-again Christian."

In the months that followed, Sammy and I took turns discipling Steve. He had a real interest in spiritual matters and wanted to grow in his faith.

About eleven months later, Steve called and wanted to know if we could have some time together. When we met, he shared that he had just learned he had cancer and was immediately beginning a treatment program.

It hardly seemed possible that my dear friend could be going through so much pain and discomfort. His spirits were high even though his condition was worsening. I will never forget the day he said, "Leonard, I want to live. I believe God could use me but if He doesn't hear me, it's okay because I know where I'm going. If I die, I want you to conduct my funeral." Many of us prayed for the Lord to heal Steve but it was not God's plan to do so.

In the fall of 1980, I was scheduled to make a trip to Eastern Europe. Just looking at Steve, I did not see how he could live until I returned. At the same time I wanted to honor his request to do his memorial service when the time came.

I was scheduled to leave on a Monday. Early Saturday morning, the telephone rang and it was his wife, Barbara, calling to let me know that he had just died. Could I have the memorial service at the ranch the next day (Sunday) in the afternoon? Can you appreciate God's timing? If it had been a day later, I would have been gone and, once behind the iron curtain, it would have been impossible for word to get through. The Bible says that "The steps of a good man are ordered of the Lord" (Psalm 37:23 KJV).

When Steve died, they pulled back the covers and his hand was resting on the Bible that Dr. Billy Graham had given him a few days earlier.

To this day I miss him but I know I will see him again and he won't be sick. He will have his resurrection body and, together with all the saints, will forever enjoy the presence and pleasures of our wonderful Lord.

Look up friends, redemption draweth nigh. The King is coming!

EIGHTEEN
MR. PRESIDENT

The Bible says, "For promotion cometh neither from the east, nor from the west, nor from the south. But God is the judge; He putteth down one, and setteth up another" (Psalm 75:6-7 KJV).

I have never been inclined to seek high office even though I have frequently found myself in a leadership role with different groups and organizations most of my life. If you could go back to my roots in a small farming community in the province of Alberta, you might wonder how likely it would be that I would achieve any of the success that has come to me. All I know is that the Lord has placed His hand on my life and given me privileges far beyond anything I could ever imagine.

One time when I was being introduced, the master of ceremonies was describing where I grew up. He said, "It's not the end of the world, but you can see it from there." A dear friend of mine was visiting that part of the world and requested his host to take him to "where Leonard grew up." Later, when I saw him, he told me that he had visited our town and the DeWitt farm, which is now devoid of human life.

He said, "Leonard, the people who said it's not

the end of the world did not tell the truth. It really is the end of the world."

I share these humorous anecdotes so you will understand how a great God can take a very ordinary person who is yielded and use that life for His glory.

In 1980, the the Lord began to put a very heavy burden on my heart for our denomination. Frequently I would find myself weeping over the needs as I perceived them.

One day the telephone rang and a dear friend who was on the Presidential Search Committee was calling. Would I be willing to let my name appear on the ballot at our next General Conference for the highest office of our denomination? My first reaction was a great outburst of laughter. He assured me the committee was very serious. Then I got scared.

I have been in love with the people of Ventura from the time we first arrived in 1971. God has blessed the church with incredible growth and the thought of leaving was almost unbearable. Also, I sensed that being President would be very lonely. It really didn't appeal to me, so I declined having my name on the ballot.

After I hung up the telephone, I reflected on what I had just experienced. I sensed the Lord speaking to me. The conversation was pretty one-sided and it went something like this: "Leonard, what did you base your answer on? You didn't even take the time to ask Me what I want. If I am really the Lord of your life, don't I have the right to deploy you wherever I choose? If I need you in Fort Wayne, Indiana, giving leadership to My church, don't I have the right to place you there or do I have to leave you in Ventura for the rest of your life? Why do you think you have had such a growing burden for the total church?"

By this time I was crying almost uncontrollably because it dawned on me that I had said no to what God was asking me to do. My pride would not permit me to pick up the telephone, call my friend back and say I had made a mistake.

The next few months were sheer agony because my burden for the church continued to increase. I knew I had closed the door on whatever role the Lord intended for me. There were days when I actually believed I was cracking up.

One evening, my godly wife said to me, "Leonard, something is wrong. You haven't been yourself for months. What is it?" Finally, I told her what had transpired. She was afraid, too, because she had no desire to leave Ventura either. Her closing remark that night was, "Leonard, no matter what we feel, you must do whatever you believe the Lord is asking you to do." As I retired for the night, I said, "Lord, I will do whatever You desire."

The next morning, moments after I arrived at my office, another friend called. He, too, was on the Presidential Search Committee. Joe told me how burdened he and his wife were for the future of the denomination. Every time they prayed, the Lord put me on their hearts. His next question was,

"Leonard, are you sure you gave the right answer several months ago?"

By then, the tears were gushing out of my eyes and I could not even answer him. Unless you have been through what I am describing, you can't imagine the awe of the moment. I had said yes to the Lord many times before but this was truly an awesome moment.

Just because I might allow my name to stand did not mean I would be elected. In many parts of the country I would be viewed as "Leonard who?" Besides, could a man from the West Coast give leadership to a strongly-based Midwestern church?

There was a great victory accomplished in my life at that point because I knew I did not love any place, person or position more than the Lord Jesus who had redeemed me years before. He truly was first in my life and that's the way we both wanted it.

Well, the rest is history. In 1981, I was elected as President of the Missionary Church and we moved to our home office in Fort Wayne, Indiana, for six wonderful years. Every good thing that has ever happened to me has been because our God is an awesome God who takes a personal interest in the lives of His people.

If you want real excitement in life, put God first. Always follow His leading and "He who has begun a good work in you will complete it until the day of Jesus Christ" (Philippians 1:6 NKJV).

He will also accomplish great things through

you. "For it is God who works in you both to will and to do for His good pleasure" (Philippians 2:13 NKJV).

To Him be all honor, glory and praise.

NINETEEN
MIRACLE FLIGHT

I have always enjoyed reading those passages of Scripture that reveal the miracle-working power of God. He is truly an awesome God who intervenes in the affairs of men and provides for His people at all times.

Reading about God's acts of power is one thing, but experiencing them is another. I praise Him that He has permitted me to personally see His mighty power at work in my life on numerous occasions.

When I was in a leadership role with the Missionary Church based in Fort Wayne, Indiana. I was frequently asked to speak at church functions. The Lord very kindly put several gifted pilots in my life who were willing to fly me to some of those speaking engagements. This made it possible for me to travel during the week and still be home in time for a good night's rest before going to the office the next day.

I was scheduled to speak in one of our churches in Kitchener, Ontario, on Thanksgiving weekend in November, 1985. One of my associates was also going but would not be returning for several days so I needed to plan a way to get home. My good friend, Rev. Mike Livingston, was pastoring our church at Grabill, Indiana. He is an excellent instrument-rated pilot. Mike had flown me to various engagements on several occasions. He agreed to come and bring me back. Monday, November 25, was a beautiful day. The forecast said there might be some light rain later in the day but we would be home before it arrived so that posed no real problem.

I was at the airport when Mike arrived in the familiar red and white Piper Cherokee. It was a terrific little plane that had carried the two of us many miles together. We enjoyed visiting with each other as we took off for Detroit Metro Airport with a certain sense of enthusiasm. It was always fun to find out what had been happening in each other's ministry.

We cleared customs in Detroit and then took to the skies once again for the short flight to Fort Wayne. The weather looked great so Mike was flying under Visual Flight Rules (VFR). Flying time to our destination should have been about one hour. As we came closer to Fort Wayne, we could see cloud formations piling up like mountains of cotton, except that some of the cotton looked soiled. Still, this should have posed no problems and, besides, we were almost home.

Then, without any warning, we found ourselves in an ice storm. In seconds the plane was covered with ice. Not being a pilot, I had no idea how serious our situation was. I always made it a practice to look at the pilot and, if he wasn't nervous, I remained calm. Outwardly Mike was the picture of a man in control.

Immediately he contacted the control tower at Toledo, Ohio, for permission to change over to Instrument Flight Rules (IFR). I thanked the Lord that Mike was instrument-rated because the windows were completely iced over. It was impossible to fly the plane visually.

Another problem we faced was that the plane did not have de-icing equipment which newer models have. In addition to that, we had no way of knowing how much ice was building up on the plane. When there is a lot of build-up, it adds extra weight to the plane and interferes with the flow of air over the wings and propeller. If the situation doesn't improve rapidly, the plane will fly more and more slowly until it stalls. Guess what comes next? They say it isn't the stalling that hurts you— it's the sudden stop on the earth below.

Mike and I were both praying. The Bible says, "My times are in Your hands" (Psalm 31:15 NIV). Sometimes we forget how special God's hands are. When we are in His hands we are safe, no matter what danger may be threatening.

Mike knew much better than I how critical our situation was. He was praying, "Lord, please don't let the pitot tube ice up." Since our flying incident, I have learned that the pitot tube is a small probe fastened to the bottom side of one of the wings. It has a small pinhole opening that faces forward. To quote my pilot, "The force of the outside air rushing past the hole creates a vacuum in the tube. This vacuum system powers several crucial flight instruments inside the plane. Two of these are the airspeed indicator and altimeter." If Mike was flying with only the instruments and the tube was clogged, he wouldn't be able to tell the plane's airspeed or altitude. The fascinating thing is that all the instruments functioned normally.

I noticed a button that read *Hot air vent* and asked Mike if he thought that would clear the windows. He shook his head 'no' indicating the ice was too thick. Only moments later, hardly thinking about what he was doing, he reached over and pulled that button out to open the vent. My spine tingles as I relate what happened next. In a few moments the ice on the windows turned to water and ran off. We were once again able to see and soon were cleared to land at the Fort Wayne Airport.

No words can describe the relief and exhilaration we both felt when those wheels touched down. This old earth is pretty great and I have a much greater appreciation for her.

When we got out of the plane, Mike ran his hands over her sleek, glistening body. Looking at me, he said, "Leonard, she's covered with ice," Actually, the plane was covered with a half-inch and the pitot tube was completely incased in ice. Yet, all the instruments had functioned perfectly.

Mike went into the hanger and brought out several knowledgeable people to examine the plane. They said, "This plane won't fly. It's totally impossible. Someone upstairs was sure looking after you. Etc."

In Isaiah 43:1-3, God said, "Fear not for I have

redeemed you; I have called you by your name; you are Mine. When you pass through the waters, I will be with you; And through the rivers, they shall not overflow you. When you walk through the fire, you shall not be burned, nor shall the flame scorch you. For I am the Lord your God, The Holy One of Israel, your Savior" (NKJV).

Dear friend, I don't know what kind of peril you may be facing but Jehovah-Jireh says you don't have to be afraid. He is more than sufficient for any crisis in your life. Trust Him today.

TWENTY
AT THE BOTTOM
OF A FIRE ESCAPE

Does the Lord really know the secret desires of our hearts? Even if He does, what value does He place on them?

When I was a boy, we used to have an annual school picnic. We played games, rolled in the fresh grass, roasted weiners and marshmallows and always had a wonderful time. For weeks before the day of the picnic, I would ask the Lord to give us good weather. I would tell Him how good I would be if He would give us a bright, sunny day. Some years it rained the very day of the picnic and it had to be called off. This was so disappointing and in my boyish faith, I wondered if God really cared.

With the passing of time, I have come to know the Lord in a more mature way. One thing I know for sure — our Heavenly Father does care about the things that concern us. The Apostle Peter knew this when he wrote, "Casting all your care on Him, for He cares for you" (1 Peter 5:7 NKJV).

As our children were growing up, we tried to instill in them those values that would ensure their happiness and by which they would please God. I am sure our daughter wondered, since she adhered to such a strict moral code, if she would ever find a fellow with similar ideals who wanted to marry her. Sometimes we may feel that we need to lower our standards or compromise in order to be liked or accepted.

Well, Pam loved us and she loved the Lord. She dated some in high school but "Mr. Right" did not appear. At the same time, the desire to one day be married and have a family never left her. She attended Azusa Pacific University and graduated from there but still the man of her dreams did not appear.

She decided it was wise to go to seminary and get her Master's degree in Christian Education. We were thrilled to have her pick Asbury Theological Seminary in Wilmore, Kentucky. Pam was every guy's best friend. They confided in her and she was like a sister to many of the young men preparing for the ministry.

One winter morning of her final year at Asbury, Pam was running late and decided to go down the fire escape rather than the crowded stairway. It wasn't very long and she could save some time. As she began her descent, suddenly her feet slipped on the frosty step and she made a very bruising, undignified trip to the bottom. I don't know which hurt worse, her pride or her body. As she lay there wondering if she could still move, a big, good-looking guy from Ohio was bending over her, asking if she was okay and then gently helping her up.

Well, you guessed it. That was the beginning of

a courtship that led to marriage and a shared
ministry for the glory of God. At just the right
time, under unique circumstances, the Lord honored
Pam by bringing Jim into her life. If we had picked
him, we couldn't be happier.

Was it worth waiting for God's choice?
Absolutely! Is she glad that she followed the high
standards of Scripture? By all means.

You see, dear friend, the counsel of Psalm 37:4 is
still true for us today: "Delight yourself in the
Lord and He will give you the desires of your
heart" (NIV). God's ways may twist or turn but
one thing is sure, He maketh no mistake. You can
afford to wait for His choice for your life.

TWENTY-ONE
WHAT A COINCIDENCE!

One of the great themes in the Bible is the existence and ministry of angels. There are different orders of angels but all are devoted to carrying out the desires of our God. They delight to do His will and serve Him. Part of God's plan is that they should care for us. I personally believe that every Christian has a guardian angel who is assigned to help us with the bumps and lumps of life. When we are in Heaven, I believe it will be revealed to us all the ways in which our guardian angels intervened in our lives. At that moment, we will be filled with awe and praise for all of God's goodness.

Let me share with you an event in which I believe either our daughter's angel or ours or both helped us deal with what could have been a very serious problem.

We were living in Fort Wayne, Indiana. Pam had completed her Master's program at Asbury Theological Seminary in Wilmore, Kentucky. She had been hired by a church on the island of Kauai to be their Director of Christian Education.

Transportation on the island would be very important. Since we knew that the Ford Mustang was in good condition, we decided to ship it from

Long Beach, California.

The car was in Fort Wayne, Indiana, which meant Pam would have to drive it across country. We did not want her to make the trip alone so we flew a close friend of hers to Indiana to make the trip with her. It might be years before they would see each other again so this would be a special time in their lives.

Plans were made for them to leave on July 4th. On the second, some relatives came in from Nebraska. On the morning of the third when I got up to go to the office, I discovered our guests had parked right in front of my garage and I could not get my car out. Rather than awaken them, I decided to drive Pam's car to work and encouraged her to use mine when she was able to get it out of the garage.

On the way to the office, our daughter's car was making the worst possible kind of noise. It was obvious she could not start out across country with it making such a racket. I drove to a service station and asked a mechanic friend what could possibly be wrong. He listened and said, "The water pump is done." When I asked if he could repair it, he informed me that this particular engine was very difficult to work on. He recommended that I call another place in the city.

After I explained my dilemma to the service manager, he discovered they had just one water pump of the kind required in stock. If I could bring the car in immediately, they would have it done by 5:00 p.m. Later in the day when I picked it up, he said, "It's a good thing you drove that car and found the problem. Those young ladies wouldn't have gone more than fifty miles and they would have been stranded by the roadside on July the fourth."

Some would say, "What a coincidence!" My response to that is, our Heavenly Father watches out for His children. He knew all about that defective water pump and saw to it that the problem was discovered and corrected before they left home.

In Psalm 121:1-2 we read, "I will lift up my eyes to the hills — From whence comes my help? My help comes from the Lord, Who made heaven and earth" (NKJV).

The songwriter was right. "My Jesus knows just what I need...my every need He supplies. He knows just what I need."

Friend, He knows what you have need of today and He will supply as you look to Him.

"What A Coincidence"   JEHOVAH-JIREH IS HIS NAME, BY LEONARD DEWITT

TWENTY-TWO
CAN YOU EVER GO BACK?

In John 14:2-3, our Lord said, "I go to prepare a place for you. And if I go and prepare a place for you, I will come again and receive you to Myself; that where I am, there you may be also" (NKJV). This promise by Jesus Christ has been a source of great comfort to His followers. It is filled with hope for all who truly love Him.

Frequently we hear the saying, "You can never go back." Is that true or are there times when God says, "I want you to go back?"

In the Old Testament, we read of Moses running away. Years later God sent him back home to his people in Egypt to undertake a great mission. See Exodus, chapters 2 and 3.

We also read of Jacob, cheating his brother out of the blessing. Years later he returned to face the music and be reconciled to his brother. See Genesis, chapters 31 to 33.

When we left Ventura in 1981 to assume a leadership role in the home office of our denomination, we had no intention or ever returning except for an occasional visit. The likelihood of a pastor returning to a former parish is very close to zero.

I was elected to a four-year term as President of the Missionary Church. Even though the Lord had put a number of burdens on my heart for the denomination, I was sure I would not be in that office for an extended period of time. One of the goals I felt very strongly about was seeing a strong commitment to reaching the lost through church planting. This vision caught on quickly and has been going strong ever since.

In 1985 I was re-elected to another four-year term. The Lord was so faithful and we saw some really significant growth take place. Organizations don't like change but the Holy Spirit helped our people to accept change and we were very encouraged. Early in 1986 I began to experience frustration because I felt a new agenda for the denomination was in place. My main activity now was serving as an administrator and public speaker. This just wasn't enough for me. As I sought the Lord for wisdom I really sensed Him saying, "You have done what I asked you to do and you are now free to serve me in other ways."

More and more I sensed I should resign mid-term but that was unheard of. Still, as I prayed, this seemed the course we should follow. The Lord put on my heart going back to the front lines to practice what I had been preaching. Thus, in the fall of 1986, I announced that we would be stepping down at our next General Conference.

The next question we confronted was: "Where can we best fulfill the vision that you, Lord, have given us for the church?" Offers came pouring in —

Vancouver, B.C.; Denver, Colorado; Pennsylvania, etc. Then telephone calls started coming form Ventura, California. The pulpit there was empty and some of the people were wondering if we would come back.

At first I did not consider the idea seriously because we wouldn't be available for almost a year. Also, I knew I had changed in the years we had been away and the church had also changed. I sincerely questioned whether a man could successfully return to a former parish. Finally, the District Superintendent of that district called and said, "Leonard, you are a candidate for that church whether you want to be or not. You must decide if you would be willing to come."

Early in 1987, I traveled to the West Coast for the denomination. I agreed to meet with members of the search committee. At that meeting, things began to churn inside of me and I sensed that it might possibly work. I started doing research and found several pastors across the land who had done this very thing. The key to its success was, "Why did you leave?" I had not been voted out. Neither had I gone to take another church. The more we prayed, the more excited we became. Another interesting piece of the picture was that we had never sold our home. That's a story in itself. The fact was, if we went back, we would have a place to live. Property values had sky-rocketed and I doubt if we could have bought into the market.

Finally, we felt a real freedom to let the people decide whether they wanted us to return. At a special business meeting, we answered as many questions as possible and then the people voted. I had determined that the vote would have to be at least ninety percent or we would not come. No one apart from my wife knew the figure that we had set. When the leaders shared that the vote was slightly over ninety-four percent, I sensed terrific joy and confirmation.

Yes, you can go back if God so directs. We are having the time of our lives. The Lord has helped us mother several new churches in strategic communities and I feel that the best days for the church are ahead.

Years ago, the Lord quickened to my heart His promise in Isaiah 45:2, "I will go before you and make the crooked places straight" (NKJV).

Jehovah-Jireh is our Provider. Let Him guide you into the very place where you can best serve Him.

TWENTY-THREE
CHRISTOPHER

This book is about miracles. It illustrates God's answers to prayers offered in faith by a family who has relied on Him again and again through the years.

When we knew that our children had been conceived, we started praying right away that the Lord would begin preparing a life partner for each of them. As I reflected on God choosing a wife for Isaac, I was quite sure He would not mind picking a husband for Pamela and a wife for Sheldon. You need to know that if we had picked our son-in-law and daughter-in-law ourselves, we could not be happier. Jim and Sheryl really fit into our family and we love them dearly.

No manuscript of mine would be complete without introducing you to Christopher, our first grandchild. He is a wonderful answer to prayer. I am including this brief chapter to offer encouragement to all those precious couples who long to be parents and, for whatever reason, God has not yet seen fit to grant their desire. Don't stop believing.

Sheldon and Sheryl had been married several years and decided it was time to start their family. After months went by and they had no success, they had tests done which showed that, because of some physical problems Sheryl had, they might never have children. This news was a very great disappointment to them and to us. Many people began to pray. It was a source of great joy to them to know that so many people cared.

In time, doctors felt that surgery might help. There were no guarantees but it was worth a try. The operation went well and was followed by months of medical therapy. Finally, the doctors said it was time for them to try again. Several more months went by and then, wonder of wonders, Sheryl was with child.

On January 5, 1989, Christopher was born. He is such a precious little boy. Now we are praying for him. We are trusting that he will grow up to be a man with a heart for God. His name means "Christ-bearer" or "Follower of Christ." God's desire is that each of us be followers of His Son every day of our lives. One of the best ways we can do this is to be men and women of faith.

Hebrews 11:6 says, "Without faith it is impossible to please Him, for he that cometh to God must believe that He is, and that He is a rewarder of them that diligently seek Him" (KJV).